ABORIGINAL

PAINTINGS

From Australia

INTRODUCTION BY

CHARLES P. MOUNTFORD

A MENTOR-UNESCO ART BOOK

PUBLISHED BY
THE NEW AMERICAN LIBRARY OF WORLD LITERATURE, INC.
BY ARRANGEMENT WITH UNESCO

FIRST PRINTING, OCTOBER, 1964

MENTOR TRADEMARK REG. U. S. PAT. OFF. AND FOREIGN COUNTRIES
REGISTERED TRADEMARK—MARCA REGISTRADA

MENTOR-UNESCO ART BOOKS ARE PUBLISHED BY
THE NEW AMERICAN LIBRARY OF WORLD LITERATURE, INC.
501 MADISON AVENUE, NEW YORK, NEW YORK 10022

PRINTED IN ITALY BY AMILCARE PIZZI S.P.A. MILANO

ABORIGINAL

PAINTINGS

Australia is of especial interest to the student of the history of art, for it is in this country alone that he can watch a Stone Age artist at work, learn from him the meaning of the designs he is using, and observe the techniques he employs. To obtain a more complete understanding of the art of the Australian aborigines, however, it would be well to examine first several of the factors that affect their economic and artistic life—for instance, the country in which they live, their simple means of gaining a livelihood, their philosophical concepts, the motifs available to them, and the effect of isolation on their art, for the aborigines have been almost entirely cut off from external cultural influences for an unknown, but probably lengthy, period.

Before the arrival of the white man, the Australian continent, even its most inhospitable deserts, was inhabited by a dark-skinned, aboriginal people. No other race had established itself on this continent, nor, at the present time, do people of this aboriginal stock live in any other part of the world.

In general, Australia is an arid land. In the northern, eastern, southern and south-eastern parts of the continent the rainfall is adequate. But in the central deserts, which occupy about one-third of the land area, this rainfall seldom exceeds ten inches a year; over vast areas, indeed, the annual rainfall is not much more than five inches. In these desert areas the struggle for existence is an arduous task as the aborigines are exclusively a hunting and food-gathering people, gaining their sustenance as Nature provides; agriculture and animal husbandry are unknown to them.

The aborigines have no permanent camps; their shelters, made of grass and bark, are discarded at the end of the rainy season, or when a tribal group moves to another hunting ground. The continual movement of these nomadic peoples in their search for food has forced them to reduce their possessions to the bare essentials necessary to support themselves. Over most of the continent, the men own little more than spears, spear-throwers, shields and boomerangs, and the women's few belongings include string, wood or bark carrying utensils, simple digging sticks, and grinding stones. Before the coming of the white man, the people wore no clothing, except along the southern and eastern coasts where they used rugs made from the skins of small marsupials to keep themselves warm. Yet although the aborigines have so few material possessions, probably fewer than any other living people, they have at the same time acquired an intimate knowledge of their land. Even in the forbidding deserts they succeed in gaining not only an adequate livelihood but also sufficient leisure to follow a rich aesthetic and ceremonial life, in which they commemorate their philosophies concerning the origin of their world.

The aborigines believe that, even before there was any life, the earth had always existed as a flat, featureless plain, extending on all sides to the edge of the universe. At some ill-defined period, poetically known as the "Dream-time", giant semi-human beings, resembling animals in their appearance but acting like men and women, rose miraculously out of the level plains under which they had been slumbering for countless ages. As these mythical beings wandered over the countryside, they created the topography: the sea coasts, the swamp-lands, the rivers and the mountain ranges.

An intimate knowledge of the mythical stories concerning this creation period is transmitted from one generation of aborigines to the next by means of the art, music and drama of their ceremonial life. Although this book deals only with the graphic art of the aborigines, in particular

that of the painter, music and drama play an equally important role in the preservation of these myths.

In this Stone Age community, whose way of life is of the simplest and whose isolation from other peoples has been of long duration, the symbols employed in the arts, particularly in the graphic arts, are in general comparatively simple. It has been asserted by some that men and women living at this stage of development are almost devoid of artistic appreciation, their thoughts rising little higher than the gathering of food and the perpetuation of their species. The research of others, however, has shown that primitive man, of which the Australian aborigine is an excellent example, is as sensitive in the creation of beauty, particularly the beauty of the graphic arts, as is any other race. The fact that the art forms of primitive man are less developed than those of more sophisticated peoples bears no relationship to the amount of pleasure enjoyed in the production of any work of art, be the artist primitive or modern. Among the Australian aborigines the arts are a living force, an integral part of the activities of the community. This is particularly true of painting, a medium in which the artist uses his skill both to transmit tribal beliefs to others and to satisfy his innate desire to produce works of beauty.

In some phases of ceremonial art, due to the rigidity of ancient laws, the number of motifs available is severely limited. This is especially noticeable in the centre of the continent where the effects of isolation are most evident. But in the secular field the artist is free to choose, from the motifs available in the community, those best suited to his purpose. This secular art, being a living force, tends to keep up to date with events. For example, among the cave paintings of the Arnhem Land plateau are pictures of steamers and pearling luggers; while side by side with the simple cave art of the desert the aborigines have painted representations of strings of camels, and men shooting kangaroos.

However, it is along the northern coasts, where the aborigines have been subjected to influences from the Indonesian and Melanesian islands, that the number of motifs is greatest and the art most vital and complex. This is especially true of Arnhem Land, the source of all the cave and bark paintings illustrated in this book. Yet even in this area the effects of isolation are evident. A comparison of Plates 17, 23 and 28, from north-eastern Arnhem Land, with Plate 16, from Groote Eylandt, shows how decisively natural barriers can influence art forms, despite the fact that this particular barrier consists only of three straits, each less than ten miles wide. The surface of the bark paintings from north-eastern Arnhem Land are covered with a series of interesting patterns, while the paintings from Groote Eylandt are almost entirely of single or grouped figures on a plain ground.

The same contrast is even more strikingly illustrated in western Arnhem Land, where the cave paintings (Plates 1 to 14) are more naturalistic and fuller of action than elsewhere in Australia. Yet on Melville Island, which is separated from western Arnhem Land by a dangerous tideway, albeit in places only fourteen miles wide, the designs on the bark paintings and burial poles are so formalized that only the artist who produced them could explain their meanings.

There is no artist class in an aboriginal community. Every man, at some time or other, will be called upon to act as the tribal artist. His task may be to engrave a sacred object, to decorate a burial pole, or to paint designs on the cave wall, the bare ground, or the body of a performer in a ceremony. In fact, all aborigines are natural artists. The author has yet to meet one who could not or did not want to paint. Moreover, all seem to have had a fully conceived mental picture before they began painting, for it is seldom that a man altered a design or even corrected a brush stroke. Some, naturally, are more gifted, but always the elements of their simple pictures are skilfully adapted to the available space, and the colours chosen with great effect. To watch these aboriginal artists at work, totally absorbed in their efforts, is to be convinced that they are experiencing the same pleasure in their creative efforts as is felt by artists of any other culture.

From these facts it can be concluded that the artistic impulse is as much an innate part of the human mind as are speech, music and dancing. In other words, man is inherently an artist; he does not need formal training. This conviction, that to produce works of art, no matter how simple, is a propensity of the human mind and that the activity is carried out for its own sake, is held by the first of the two shools of thought on the function of art in a primitive society. The other school takes the opposite view. It believes that primitive man is essentially practical, and that he paints, say, a snake on the walls of a cave, not because he gains any pleasure in the act, but because he believes that by so doing he can make the snakes reproduce in greater numbers.

The research of the author, over many years, into the art of the aborigines has convinced him that both factors are present. Art is used by every member of the tribe to satisfy his innate desires, and by the tribal magicians to control the forces of nature, increase the food supply, punish wrong-doers or destroy enemies.

The art of the Australian aborigines can be classified under three headings: engraving, sculpture, and painting. The first two forms will be dealt with briefly, leaving the richer field of the painter for more detailed study.

The aboriginal engravers use their skill in decorating their shields, boomerangs, and spear-throwers; in depicting the mythical stories on their sacred objects of wood and stone; in making the elaborate patterns on the tree-trunks and hard surfaces of their Bora ceremonial ground; and in carving simple designs in the rock surfaces.

Among the finest examples of this form of art are the intricate patterns, of great beauty, engraved on the wooden shields of eastern and south-eastern Australia. In north-western Australia the aborigines also display considerable skill in the decoration of the sacred boards and pearl-shell ornaments. On these the artists often engrave the complicated, interlocking key pattern that was once used in the ceramic art of ancient Greece. In central Australia the motifs engraved on the sacred objects are much simpler than those used elsewhere, but nevertheless the artistry displayed in their placing gives them a simple beauty of their own.

The art of sculpturing and modelling figures of men and creatures is unevenly but widely spread throughout Australia, being most highly developed on the northern coasts where the aborigines have been subject to occasional influences from Papua and Indonesia. In both Cape York and Arnhem Land, the aborigines carve wooden heads and full-length figures representing mythical people at the time of the Creation, as well as the creatures of their everyday life; while in western Arnhem Land they are most expert in modelling human heads in clay and ochre. Some of the aboriginal figures from north-western Australia, carved in wood and stone, are equal in workmanship and artistic quality to those in Arnhem Land. So far as is known, only two examples of carved figures from southern Australia have been preserved in museum collections; one is a well-formed head on the handle of a spear-thrower, and the other a face on a wooden water bucket.

The most important factor in the aesthetic life of the Australian aborigines is, however, the art of the painter. The decoration of the sacred objects belonging to the rituals of the men, the ornamentation of the weapons and implements of everyday life, the painting of large and elaborate patterns on the ground at the time of certain totemic ceremonies, the designs on the burial poles (as well as the complex body patterns of the performers) in the spectacular mourning ceremonies of Melville Island, all bear witness to the aesthetic importance of the aboriginal painter.

The most beautiful examples of aboriginal graphic art are, without doubt, the cave and bark paintings. In Australia, paintings are found only in shallow caves and rock shelters, for (unlike Palaeolithic man in Europe) the aborigine does not decorate rock surfaces far removed from the light of day. These cave paintings are widespread, but their distribution is irregular due to the fact that their existence depends largely on the availability of rock shelters to act as protection from the wind and rain. Yet it is a curious fact that there are no recorded cave paintings in either Tasmania or south-eastern Australia, although in these mountainous areas there must be numerous places suitable for cave painting sites.

The motifs of cave paintings differ considerably. They are simple in the southern and central areas of the continent and become increasingly complex until they reach their highest development along the northern coasts.

In the Kimberly Ranges, in north-western Australia, there are two unusual art forms depicting human beings—the large Wandjina paintings and the small Giro-Giro figures.

The Wandjina paintings are remarkable for their size, one recorded example being eighteen feet in length, and for their white, mouthless faces, surrounded by one or two horseshoe-shaped bows, with lines radiating from the outer symbol. The aborigines believe that during the early days of the world, each Wandjina (and there were many) created the topography of one particular area. His task completed, the Wandjina transformed himself into a mythical snake and entered a nearby waterhole. But before doing so, he left his image, in the form of a cave painting, in an adjacent rock shelter and decreed that, before the start of each monsoon season, the aborigines must renovate the cave painting. The renovating of the Wandjina cave paintings not only causes the monsoon rains to start (a welcome change after the hot and arid season) but also ensures the thriving and increase of the food animals and plants. The disregarding of the law of renovation brings drought and hunger in its train. When the paintings in the cave grow dim the Wandjina vanishes, and with the Wandjina go rain and fertility.

On the other hand, the aborigines explain that the little Giro-Giro drawings, often only a few inches in height and painted entirely in red, are the work not of living men at all, but of a fairy or spirit people, also called the Giro-Giro, who live in the surrounding forest. The art of the Giro-Giro always depicts men and women in action, an antithesis to the tall, static figures of the Wandjina.

By far the most colourful examples of cave art in

Australia are found along the western edge of the Arnhem Land plateau. There, as in north-western Australia, are two unrelated art forms: the curious "X-ray" paintings of the aborigines, and the single-line drawings of the Mimis, a fairy people who, according to the aborigines, still live among the rocks of the plateau. In "X-ray art" the aborigine paints not only what he sees (that is, the external form of the human being or creature) but also what he knows to be there, though unseen—the skeleton, heart, lungs, stomach, and other internal details. Although this remarkable art is used, in simple forms, by native people in other parts of the world, in no other part of Australia nor anywhere else are the examples so skilfully produced as in the caves of western Arnhem Land. In that locality some of the cave paintings of fish, up to eight feet in length and composed of hundreds of red, yellow and white lines, are among the most beautiful examples of Australian cave art.

In contrast, the small, single-line drawings credited by the aborigines to the Mimi artists have a feeling for composition and movement entirely lacking in the work of the X-ray artists. The only subject of Mimi art is man in action—man dancing, running, fighting, throwing spears. These Mimi artists are reputed to live under the great rocks of the plateau. They are particularly tall and thin, so thin in fact that they do not hunt in stormy weather, fearing that if they did so the wind would break their frail bodies. No aborigine has ever actually seen a Mimi, for these spirit people are so gifted with both keen sight and hearing that they can at once detect the approach of an intruder, and escape from him into their rocky homes. Without doubt, the aborigines are attempting to explain through this myth of the Mimis the presence of an art form they themselves do not practise. There is no evidence, however, that the so-called Mimis were other than aborigines.

Plate 14, the example of X-ray art chosen for inclusion in this book, pictures a large fish, probably a sweep (*Scorpus aequipinnis*). The anatomical details of this creature are well defined: the backbone, the gills (the two groups of parallel lines leading from the head to the stomach), and the swim bladder (the large red oval in the body of the fish).

The remaining cave paintings illustrated show some of the spirit people of western Arnhem Land. They are of two kinds: the Mamandis, dangerous and ill-disposed toward the native people, and the Mimis, who do not interfere with anyone. At the time the author discovered these paintings, his aboriginal informants explained to him both their meanings and the beliefs associated with them.

These spirit people live in the country along the western edge of the Arnhem Land plateau. Their homes are among the boulders of the rocky hills, in the water-holes of the flood-plains, in the termite mounds, the hollow trees and the dense, fresh-water jungles. Although both the dwelling-places and the characteristics of each of the spirit people are well known to the aborigines, they have never been seen. But it is believed that the more dangerous of them are visible to the medicine men, who try to hunt them away before they can harm anyone.

Plate 1 illustrates a family of harmless spirit people, the Nalbidji. In the centre are three men wearing feathered head-dresses and arm-bands. Each man has a spear-thrower in one hand, a single spear in the other, and a sacred carrying bag over his shoulder. At the extreme left and upper right of this group are two women, and at the lower left of the illustration is a sacred object, wrapped in paper-bark and tied with string.

Part of an interesting frieze, some fifteen feet long, is shown in Plate 2; it represents a group of running Mimis, most of them carrying spears and spear-throwers. The triangular objects in the hands of the first two men are fans made from the wing of a goose. The tall female figures, in red, symbolize two of the much-feared Nama-rakain spirit people, who, by means of the string held between their fingers, are able to travel from place to place in their search for human victims. There are both male and female Namarakain. When a Namarakain knows where a sick aborigine is encamped, he sneaks up, drags the spirit from the victim's body and leaves him to die.

An aborigine renovating a cave painting of the serpent Yarapi.
Nama, central Australia.

The Namarakain can be seen only by the medicine men, whose duty it is to keep these evil spirits away from all sick people.

In Plate 3 appears an attractive group of tall-bodied people, two of whom have been painted over the faded image of a sea-going turtle. The aborigines could not explain the significance of the recumbent figure on the lower left.

An aboriginal ceremony is pictured in Plate 4. The two men at the extreme left are providing the music for the dance, one blowing a long wooden trumpet or drone tube, and the other beating the music sticks. The large central figure with spears, a spear-thrower and a fan is leading the dance, in which the remainder of the men are taking part. A portion of the group at the right-hand side has been obliterated by running water.

In Plate 5 are a number of Nalbidji spirit people engaged in a kangaroo hunt. At the upper right is a seated man with a woman standing beside him. Between the kangaroos there is a group of two women and two men, one of whom has speared the creature in the front of him.

A well-composed and unusual panel of cave paintings which, according to the informants, were self-portraits of the Mimi people is shown in Plate 6. The tall, graceful Mimi in the centre has been painted over a well-drawn spear-man who is carrying a goose-wing fan. At the right is a Mimi woman, with a stick in her hand, and at the upper left, a heterogeneous group of human beings. Many partly eroded paintings can be seen in the background.

Considerable skill must have been necessary to paint the delicate figures in Plate 7 on the cave ceiling. Each of the two skilfully-drawn Mimis, in elaborate head-dresses, has a long spear and a spear-thrower in one hand, and a bundle of short spears and a goose-wing fan in the other.

Plate 8 is a drawing of a Mimi with protruding lips which, it was explained, indicated that he was laughing. This spirit man has decorations on his elbows, a spear-thrower in one hand, multi-barbed spears and a goose-wing fan in the other, and is carrying a bag suspended from his neck.

The form and arrangement of the four running women in Plate 9 and the strong sense of movement that pervades the whole composition, makes this painting one of the outstanding examples of Australian cave art. These women were identified as one or another of the Mimis, although the aborigines could not remember their specific names.

Plate 10 depicts a distorted group of the dangerous Namarakain people, painted on the ceiling of a low cave. The woman at the top is carrying the loop of string with which, as mentioned above, she can travel from place to place. Three of the remaining figures, one a male, are complete, but the painting at the extreme left could not be identified.

In a remarkable drawing of three dangerous Mamandi spirit people (Plate 11), the Mimi artist has shown a richness of imagination not often seen in Australian cave art. The man on the left is sub-incised, and the one in the middle, circumcised. The figure at the right is bisexual; the body is divided at the circular head, the left-hand side being male, and the right female. With each figure the artist has used different motifs for the hands, feet and head, while the bodies are so interwined that their details are not evident on first examination.

A Mimi woman with large feet and hands, and wearing a curious form of head-dress, is illustrated in Plate 12. On the right is a fresh-water cat-fish.

Plate 13 portrays a dangerous Mamandi called Adungun, who travels about the country killing the aborigines and eating them. The leading figure is Adungun, his abdomen full of dead people. He carries spears and a spear-thrower in his hands, and a honey-bag is suspended from his shoulder. Adungun is being pursued by an aboriginal who has tried but failed to spear him.

The art of painting on bark appears to have been practised in Australia wherever the aborigines used that material to construct their wet-weather shelters. Though this art form was used by the native people both of Tasmania and of the southern and eastern coasts, it was not practised in the centre of the continent, possibly because the low rainfall of that area and the nomadic

17

An aboriginal artist at work. Yirkalla, north-eastern Arnhem Land.

habits of its people made even semi-permanent camps unnecessary.

An examination of the lamentably few bark paintings from southern Australia preserved in museum collections shows that the motifs employed are simple. But it is in the far north, and particularly in Arnhem Land and the adjacent islands, that the aborigines have become most skilled in the production of this art form.

In general, painting on sheets of bark is a secular activity, from which the men of Arnhem Land gain much aesthetic satisfaction. But as the life and thought of these artists are so dominated by myths explaining the origin of their world, their bark paintings deal almost entirely with the stories of Creation. The majority of the bark paintings can be seen by the women and children, but there are some which belong exclusively to the esoteric life of the men. To ensure their secrecy, these paintings are destroyed immediately the rituals are completed.

The bark paintings illustrated in this book were produced by the aborigines of five localities (Yirkalla and Milingimbi in the north-eastern corner of Arnhem Land, Oenpelli and Goulburn Island along the northern edge, and Groote Eylandt in the Gulf of Carpentaria). There is considerable variation in the art forms: those from the north-eastern sector are made up of a wide range of abstract and naturalistic designs, interestingly composed, often on colourful, cross-hatched backgrounds, while the examples from northern Arnhem Land and Groote Eylandt consist largely of single or grouped figures on a plain ground. These differences can be seen clearly by a comparison of Plates 17, 23 and 28, from Yirkalla, with Plates 25, 26 and 27, from Oenpelli, and Plate 16, from Groote Eylandt.

The colours used in bark painting are made from red, yellow, black, and white pigments which are ground, with water, on coarse-textured flat stones until they are of a cream-like consistency. Some of the pigments are obtained locally, others by trade, often over considerable distances. For a fixative the artists utilize the sap from the broken bulb of one of the tree orchids. On most occasions this sap is rubbed on the inner surface of the bark sheet, although at Groote Eylandt it is often mixed with the pigments on the grinding stone.

Three kinds of brushes are used: a narrow strip of bark, chewed at one end, for the broad lines; a thin cylindrical stick for the dots; and a flexible brush, made from either a few fibres of palm leaf or a single small feather, for the fine parallel lines. With this flexible brush held delicately between the fingers the aborigine is able to produce the fine cross-hatched backgrounds typical of the bark paintings of north-eastern Arnhem Land.

In this book there are four bark paintings from Yirkalla (Plates 17, 22, 23 and 28) and four from Milingimbi (Plates 18, 19, 20 and 24).

Plate 17 illustrates a myth which tells how one of the creators of the world tired of being a human being, transformed himself into the tiger shark Mana, and tried to make his home in a fresh-water swamp. But, finding the water too shallow, Mana entered the sea where, in company with another tiger shark, he has continued to live. Mana appears at the top of the bark painting, and at the bottom is his companion; the wavy lines at their tails indicate the wakes they create as they move through the water. The squares in the upper and lower panels symbolize dead leaves resting on the surface of the swamp.

In Plate 22 are a number of sea-creatures. There is little doubt that the painting illustrates some mythical story. The two large figures at the upper left are devil-rays, and that at the right is a canoe containing three turtles. At the bottom is a group of water creatures, including a frog, a sting-ray, a fish, a sea-going turtle, etc. Scattered through the painting are a number of octopi, which according to aboriginal myth are the friends of the devil-ray. It is likely that the rectangular designs refer to totemic places belonging to the sea-creatures.

The left-hand painting in Plate 23 illustrates part of an extensive myth dealing with the adventures of Mura-Mura, a mythical man famous for his skill in catching fish. In one hand he holds four fish, in the other, a twin-barbed spear with which he has transfixed still another fish. At the top of the painting, Mura-Mura is asleep under a tree with his catch of fish cooking on the fire beside him. A number of mythical sea-creatures which thrived during the early days of the world appear in the right-hand painting in Plate 23. Their home is now at the bottom of the sea between Cape Arnhem and Port Bradshaw, on the western shore of the Gulf of Carpentaria. In the lower panel are four octopi and a sea-going turtle and in the upper, three queen-fish and three octopi. The rectangular figure at the upper right is a totemic rock on the bottom of the sea. A queen-fish is resting on this rock, and two octopi have attached themselves to its base.

The bark painting shown in Plate 28 is an aboriginal conception of a wet season seascape. In the upper panel three thunderclouds are drifting across the sky. The dark-coloured bases of the two on the right indicate they have not yet shed their rain, but in the one on the left, the storm has almost expended itself, although the rain is still falling. The lower panel depicts the open sea, viewed from above. The dark-coloured cross-hatched areas portray the sand and the lighter represent the sea-water. The creatures are sting-rays feeding along the bottom. The crescents on their bodies indicate masses of fat, a food much enjoyed by the aborigines.

No details were collected of the four Milingimbi bark paintings (Plates 18, 19, 20 and 24), except that they are associated, in some way, with the extensive myth of the Djunkgao sisters who during the early days of the world created much of the topography of Arnhem Land. These four paintings are, however, excellent examples of the attractive cross-hatched patterns produced by the artists of Milingimbi.

The bark paintings from Oenpelli (Plates 25, 26 and 27) and those from Goulburn Island (Plates 15 and 21) belong to the art of northern Arnhem Land.

At the left of Plate 25 is painted the little spirit man, Dignuk, who catches his fish during the hours of darkness in the shallow waters of one of the lagoons at Oenpelli. He is friendly towards the aborigines and never attacks them, although if they spear too many fish in his lagoon

Dignuk will take the remainder to another locality. The painting on the right-hand side of Plate 25 shows two of the dangerous Namarakain spirit people of whom the aborigines of Oenpelli are afraid. The male on the right has long ears which enable him to detect more readily the approach of a stranger.

The lower half of Plate 26 is an X-ray painting of the mythical kangaroo, Kandarik. He is wearing a feather-like head-dress and holding in his paws the beating stick with which he taught the aborigines to dance. The artist has indicated the brains, lungs, heart, intestines and backbone. Wili-Wilia, a little Mimi spirit man who lives by himself in a dense fresh-water jungle at the foot of the Arnhem Land plateau, appears in the top half of Plate 26. This painting shows how Wili-Wilia, by using the tree as a shelter, has crept to within spear-range of two kangaroos, and killed one of them. Both kangaroos are excellent examples of X-ray art.

Plate 27 illustrates two of the harmless spirit people, Eradbatli and Kumail-Kumail, decorated to take part in a ceremony. Eradbatli (at the right), wearing a head-dress of twigs, is a rare example of the human figure in X-ray art. The painting shows the upper and lower intestines, the spine, and the bones of the arms and legs. The cross-hatching on the chest of Eradbatli symbolizes his stomach. There are few such details in the other figure, the cross-hatching on Kumail-Kumail indicating body decorations.

Plate 15 is an interesting bark painting from Goulburn Island, depicting an edible yam with its tubers buried deep in the ground, and its vines climbing in the open air. These vines are indicated by the meandering lines, and their leaves by the arrow-shaped symbols.

Plate 21, also from Goulburn Island, pictures a spiny ant-eater (echidna), one of the two egg-laying mammals. The creature is shown with both eyes on one side of its head; its powerful digging claw is clearly visible on the hind foot, and a series of parallel lines simulate its long spines.

The aborigines of Arnhem Land, whose knowledge of the night sky is greater than that of most white men, have surrounded the constellations, and in some cases groups of smaller stars, with many strange beliefs. To them, the sun is a woman, and the moon a man. The Milky Way is a celestial river on which, every night, the sky people embark in their canoes to gather their food, the fish and the water-lily bulbs, from its waters.

The myths about Orion are varied and widespread. The Groote Eylandt aborigines look upon the constellation of Orion as a number of fishermen with the Pleiades as their wives. The three larger stars in the bark painting at the bottom left of Plate 16 illustrate these celestial fishermen (the Burumburumrunya) and the horizontal line of stars out to the left depicts the fish they have caught. At the right of the painting, the women of the Pleiades are resting in their grass hut.

The painting in the upper half of Plate 16 is an excellent example of the fine brushwork of which the Groote Eylandt men are capable. It illustrates two mythical beings, the Unwala, who when they were men created many of natural features along the coasts of Groote Eylandt and the adjoining mainland. On finishing their work the Unwala transformed themselves into mangrove crabs.

The illustrations in this book show that, although the aborigines of Arnhem Land follow an unprogressive way of life, with limited tools and equipment and simple art materials and techniques, yet their pictures, on the walls of caves and on sheets of bark, conform to the same principles of line, colour, and balance of spacing of design elements which characterize all good art, whether it be primitive or modern.

When studying the art of the aborigines of the southern and central parts of the continent, where the effects of cultural influences are at a minimum, one question inevitably arises. Has the art of Arnhem Land developed from such simple forms as the circles, crescents, meandering and straight lines used on the sacred objects of central Australia, or is it necessary to search elsewhere for its origins? For, though it is known that the art of the northern coasts has been enriched by influences from

Melanesia and Indonesia, research has not yet established how much of this northern art is basically Australian, and how much has been borrowed from external sources.

The study of the art of the native peoples of Australia is still far from complete, though the broad pattern of its motifs and their distribution has been recorded. Unfortunately, far less is known about the meaning of the living art and its associated mythical stories.

The need for research into all aspects of aboriginal art, particularly the living art, is urgent. White civilization is overwhelming the culture of these native peoples at such an alarming rate that, even within the span of the next generation, few aborigines will still be using their ancient symbols. Therefore it is essential that research should concentrate on recording all aspects of the graphic arts of the aborigines of Australia without delay, before the opportunity to do so has gone for ever.

ILLUSTRATIONS

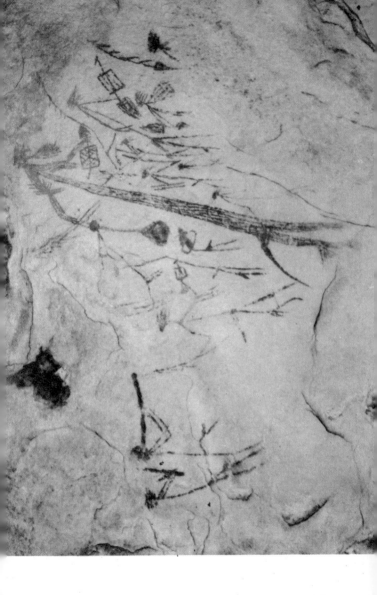

4

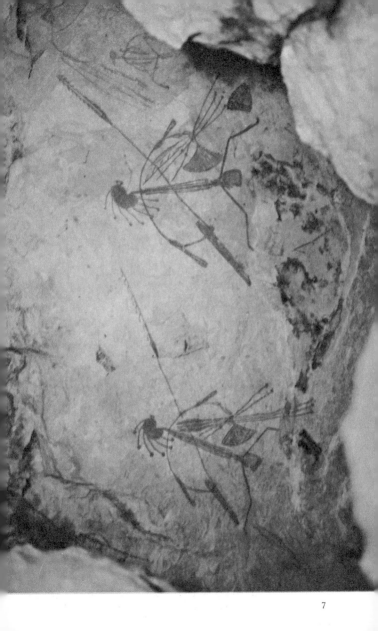

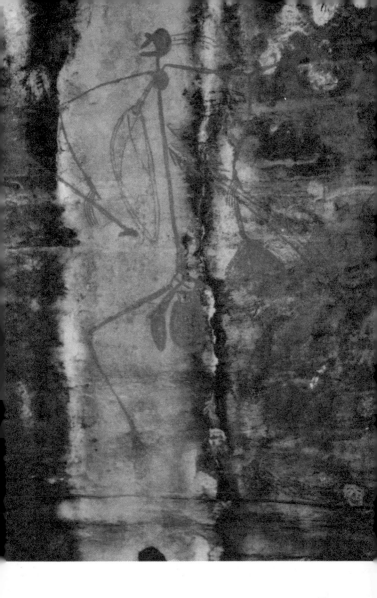

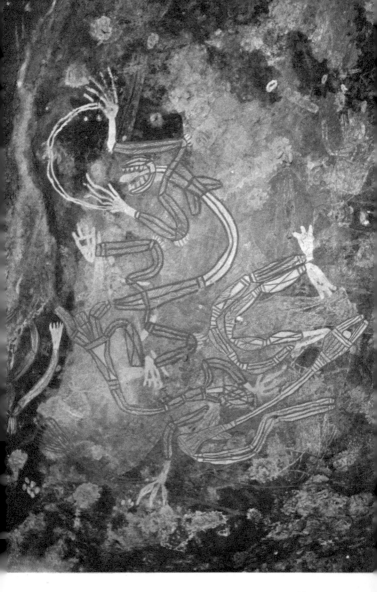

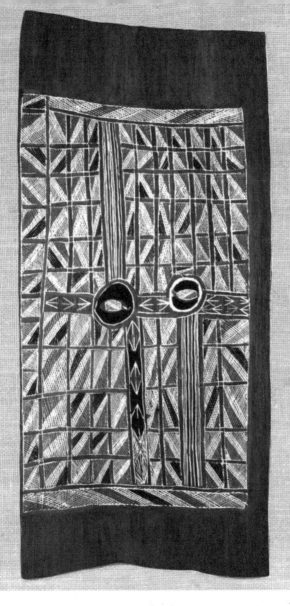

19

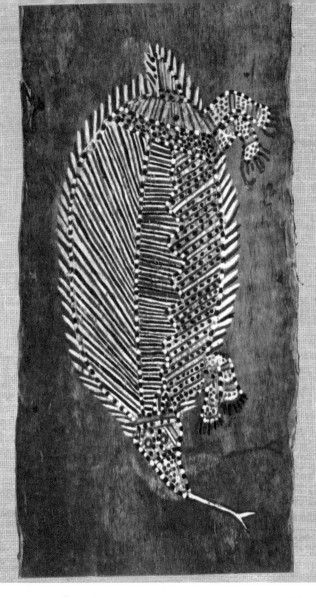

24

CONTENTS